D1784755

HOW TO PLAN YOUR PERFECT WEDDING

A Stress-Free Guide to Designing Your Big Day

Katherine Holt

Copyright © 2019 Katherine Holt
Published: August 2019

The right of Katherine Holt to be identified as author
of this Work has been asserted by her in accordance
with sections 77 and 78 of the Copyright, Designs
and Patents Act 1988.

All rights reserved. No part of this publication may be
reproduced, stored in retrieval system, copied in any
form or by any means, electronic, mechanical,
photocopying, recording or otherwise transmitted
without written permission from the publisher. You
must not circulate this book in any format.

www.giftast.com
All rights reserved.
ISBN: 9781088602737

For Adam, Marley and Tessa.

With grateful thanks to all the suppliers featured in this book - your knowledge, help and support have been invaluable.

CONTENTS

SECTION 1

SECTION 2

SECTION 3

SECTION ONE
Getting to know you.

INTRODUCTION

You're engaged. Congratulations! You're on top of the world, dreaming of your big day, and the happiness of spending the rest of your life with the one you love more than anyone else. There are magazines to buy, Pinterest boards to make, and wedding day outfits to dream of. Life is a whirlwind of congratulations, celebratory catch-ups and general happiness, leaving you wishing peace and goodwill to all humanity.

But then... reality kicks in. After a few days/weeks/years of basking in the glow of your own happiness, you realise that if you want to actually get married, you'll need to start planning. And boy, is there a lot to do.

So, like anything you want to know more about, you Google it.

Woah, that's a lot of lists.

Lists of things you should have, things you apparently need, and things you've never seen at a single wedding you've attended, but are described as a *must have*. Everyone wants to sell you something, and costs start to mount in your head, spiralling out of control before you've even spent a penny.

If you're feeling overwhelmed, and like there simply aren't enough hours in the day, then this book is for you. Don't let the overwhelm get you down - you can do it, and it will all be worth it. And don't forget, you aren't in this alone.

Together, in the pages of this book, we are going to work through your options. We're going to look at ways you can decide what you do and don't want, as well as the things you - and I mean you personally - absolutely have to have.

Disclaimer: The world of weddings is a large one, and since we're going to be looking at *your* wedding, which will be unique to you and like no other, then there's no way I can cover everything. This book will hopefully serve as a starting point for you, to help streamline the process of creating your dream wedding, as well as a handy tool to refer back to.

Because here's the thing - there's no reason that wedding planning has to be all that stressful. We expect it to be, and it doesn't disappoint us. From information overwhelm on Google to spiraling costs, and fear of upsetting not only the in-laws, but also your partner's third cousin who you've never met.

But never fear, I'm going to introduce you to some methods which will help make decision making a breeze, and cut down your worries. All of these methods are ones I've tried and tested, and I'll be telling you more about why the hell you should listen to me, in the next chapter.

Wedding Planning can - and arguably should - be fun, romantic, and just as enjoyable as that first flush of happiness you had when you became engaged. This is just another part of your journey with your partner, and just like anything else you do together, it can be filled with love and laughter.

So let's get started. As you work your way through this book, you may not find that every tip I give you is quite your thing. The important thing is to try things, and make use of what works for you, and then you'll be well on the way to feeling a lot more chilled out about this whole wedding thing.

I'm going to keep this as brief and succinct as possible. You've got a lot on - that's why you're here. I'm not going to take up loads of your time with too much unnecessary fluff.

I'm also not going to talk about legal stuff. Given that I'm based in the UK, that laws change and that this is not where my experience lies, I'll give that a wide berth. Google is your friend here, and if you're in the UK, this government website is a good place to start:

https://www.gov.uk/browse/births-deaths-marriages/marriage-divorce

There will be a fair few online resources highlighted in the book, where you can download some helpful items. You can find all of these here:

https://giftast.com/how-to-plan-your-perfect-wedding

You can also join the Facebook Group, where you can chat with others who are working on their wedding planning journey.

https://www.facebook.com/groups/planyourperfectwedding/

WHO AM I, AND WHY SHOULD YOU CARE WHAT I THINK?

Hi, I'm Katherine!

I'm your guide on this journey towards wedded bliss. I run Giftast Wedding & Event Stationery, and my job is to work with couples to create romantic, personalised wedding stationery which helps take the stress out of their wedding planning. You'll find out more about what that means and how I do it as we go on.

I'm passionate about romance, and actively work against stress and overwhelm. In my career I've worked hard to minimize the effect that is has on all aspects of my life - from the office to home, from relationships to chores.

If you want to know more about the human behind the book, you can find me on Instagram and Facebook, @giftast, or on www.giftast.com.

What do I know about all this?

Well, in a former life I was an Exec PA at a FTSE 100 company, and managed the time of some of the most disorganised people you can imagine. I have balanced working full time and planning a wedding, with starting a business and writing books. And most importantly, I'm an organising addict. I am addicted to getting things done, so I know what works.

I used to find it really difficult to get as much as I wanted to done -

I still do, but that's because the standards I set for myself are ridiculous. But then I realised that while I was really good at organising other people's lives, I wasn't applying those same practices to my own life. I was acting as though my things were so much less important than those of the people I was working for.

I became my own Exec PA, because it might not be important to anyone else if I don't remember to set up my coffee machine the night before, but it will make a massive difference to my morning.

My jobs - your jobs - which are unpaid and only for our benefit are just as important as those which we are paid to do. You are worth organising your time and worth treating yourself with the respect you give those you work for, and those you love.

WHY I CARE ABOUT YOUR WEDDING - MY DISAPPOINTING DAY

I'm not going to bore you with any extensive back story, have no fear. But I do want to share the experience of my own day, and my own wedding planning issues, so you can avoid making the same mistakes I did.

To start, let me just say this:

I love being married. Marrying my husband was the best decision I ever made, and I am so happy that we tied the knot.

But my wedding day itself? Not so much.

What went wrong?

I won't be alone in having a complicated family situation. Every family is different, and each family has its own difficulties.

We had the sadness of losing my mother-in-law just over a year before our wedding, and we knew that there was always going to be that space where she should be - that gap that only she could have filled. I won't dwell on the pain my husband and I felt at not having her at our wedding. If you've lost a loved one, you know, and you don't need me to re-live it with you.

To make things more difficult, I am completely and unrepentantly estranged from my own family. It's something I have dealt with over the past few years, and in my situation, it was and remains the best thing for me.

However, that doesn't make weddings any easier. I'd found it difficult attending other people's weddings, and I knew that planning my own would be even harder.

I have struggled through the weddings of friends, as their mothers and fathers proudly toasted them. I've been bought shots at bars by newly made in-laws, ecstatic at the happiness of their freshly extended family.

And I knew that I'd never have that. I've not missed my family, but I have missed what I wished they could be.

That perfect ideal that I saw a snapshot of at a wedding, in a father-of-the-bride speech, in the father-daughter dance. In the tears of the bride's mother, who was so proud of what her daughter had become. The stories about buying the dress.

I knew that I couldn't have any of that.

That hurt wasn't going away any time soon, and I wasn't about to wait for it to maybe get better before I married my husband.

Even though, fundamentally, a wedding is about the couple getting married, there is so much family in there. From choosing the dress, to being walked down the aisle, to the family photographs. From the moment we became engaged, I was asked how my parents liked it, and how they liked my husband-to-be, who they've barely met. Would they be paying for any of it, would they be helping me with the planning?

It hurts, and it's hard.

Whether you are estranged by choice, or have been pushed out of your own family, it's difficult to deal with the questions. More so when some people, no doubt well meaning, (to give them the benefit of the doubt), question your decisions.

"But it's your wedding! Surely you want them there!"

"This might be a good time to extend the olive branch."

"Really? Are you sure you don't want your parents there? You might regret that."

Much though I (don't) love unsolicited advice from people I barely know, it can't be helped. It's part and parcel of your wedding experience. Whether by chance or design, anybody who isn't there and would, generally, be expected to be there, will likely be mentioned by someone. Whether it's the photographer taking the pictures ("Can we have one with the bride's family now?") or just the feeling that, throughout the day, guests who didn't know me that well were wondering why I was alone, and why I was so unlovable.

I'm not unlovable, I'm great, but sometimes you just can't help but think it.

I dreaded the questions. I dreaded my wedding, but I wanted so very, very much, to marry my husband.

So, for many, many reasons, we went small. Really, we wanted to elope, but nobody we knew had, and we weren't sure how. We were worried we'd upset the people who expected to come. This led to...

Mistake 1: We made our wedding about other people.

Sure, we made it our way a bit. It was an unusual setup. We didn't want a big do, we didn't want it to last all day. We just wanted to be married. So we had a morning wedding, on a Friday, at a registry office. We thought that way, people who weren't bothered about coming could just… not. Then, a buffet lunch at a local pub, where my husband and I both did a speech, and then we left! At 3pm we went on honeymoon. Honestly, no regrets about that bit. The happiest part of my wedding day was at 9pm that night, cooking pesto pasta with my new husband in a freezing cold cottage in Wales.

Then, alone together with a glass of prosecco and a big pan of carbs, I really felt the pure bliss of being married. And the relief at it all being over.

But we had worried and pondered - will this person mind not having a plus one? Will this person like this person? Will they mind having a vegan cake? Should we have children there? (We did, and we shouldn't have.)

Mistake 2: We tried to minimise old traditions instead of making our own new ones.

I was dreading buying a dress. I didn't want to go to a bridal shop and have the champagne and the lovely staff asking questions about my family. I didn't want to take my bridesmaid and have her drink alone while I tried on dress after dress. So I bought it online, tried it on in secret, showed no-one, and made the alterations myself. The first time anyone saw it on me was the morning of my wedding. And I was proud of it, but in trying to minimise what I knew would be the bad bits of the experience, I inadvertently made the whole thing about the gap they left behind.

My dress was lovely, by the way. I love it, and it was perfect for me. It fit like a glove. But it could have been so much easier. With hindsight, there was no reason for me not to shop with my husband-to-be. Neither of us believed the superstition, and he is the one person I know guaranteed not to mind looking at me dolled up in various fancy frocks.

I wanted to pretend I was having what I thought of as "a normal wedding", even though it made things more difficult for me. I wish I hadn't done that.

Mistake 3: We didn't consider all our options

For our own reasons, my husband and I both saw the wedding day as something to be got through, rather than something to be enjoyed. We went through the motions of the wedding we thought we were supposed to have with a grim determination, consoling ourselves with the fact that it would soon be over.

But it didn't have to be that way. We could have eloped! We would have been forgiven. We could have done any number of things which would have made our wedding day what we wanted it to be, but we didn't think we could.

And you know what? For all my careful planning, things still went wrong.

Because here's the thing:

Things will go wrong at your wedding.

And, most likely, you'll be fine with it. I don't care that the venue messed up playing the music we'd spent hours choosing. I don't care that they read the wrong vows, even though we confirmed them before the ceremony. I don't care that the receptionist was rude to me when I arrived very early, because the guy driving me wouldn't listen when I told him I didn't need to set off yet. I don't care that after we were pronounced man and wife, the registrar announced me as Mrs *Husband's surname* even though I was keeping my own name, and he hadn't bothered checking.

OK, I care a bit. But so much less than I regret that we were even in that position at all. If I've learned anything from my disappointing wedding, it's that what we did was wrong for us, and to be honest, I don't think anyone enjoyed it all that much.

What we should have done:

- Elope. With my father-in-law and my best friend. Done.
- Spent the entire day together. We should have got ready together.

- Our cake was amazing, so I would still get the full cake even though we would have had a lot less guests.
- We should have chosen my dress together. Or just not had a wedding dress. I had some lovely dresses I could have worn instead. It didn't matter to me, but I made it matter, and that made me sad.

And one day I want to do all that, to renew our vows. It would be nice to have a wedding day I'm happy to remember. It would be nice not to have a wedding day where I went and hid in the toilets alone twice just to get through the stress of it.

So there you go. I had a disappointing wedding, so you don't have to!

If you don't know this already - and perhaps you do - there isn't one way to have a wedding. There isn't a right way you should be doing things. There isn't a tick list of things that you, yes - *you* - definitely need and which your wedding will fail without.* With this book, I can help you figure out what matters to you and your partner, and what you really don't care about at all.

*Other than legal stuff.

DEALING WITH DIFFICULT THINGS

So, let's get to it. There are almost certainly going to be difficulties you face as you start planning your wedding. There may be things you've put off thinking about, because you've been enjoying being in love.

These things can range from finances, through to family and anything in between. I'm not going to suggest here that I can solve your problems, but what I will say is that this is an opportunity for you and your Partner to face these things together.

If you know there is an aspect of wedding planning, or the wedding day itself which may cause one or both of you pain, the best thing you can do for yourselves now, is to own it. Your wedding is about both of you, and you need to be honest with yourself about the things you will find difficult.

Once you own the problems you'll be facing together, you can figure out how to make them work for you.

Just like my own family issues and the way I just tried to ignore how, for example, I'd feel about dress-shopping. By trying to minimise the problem, I just isolated myself further and made it more, not less of an ordeal. There are traditions which will be difficult for you, but you don't necessarily need to do them.

I felt trapped by the rigid system of weddings, the ideal that we see on TV. I wanted so badly to have that experience of crying, caring female relatives and bridesmaids in the dress shop, with champagne. But it was never going to be mine. Even if I wasn't estranged, that wasn't a relationship I had. All I thought about was how to minimise my pain at this experience, not how to make it so it was joyous for me in a different way.

When you're facing things in wedding planning which you know will cause you pain, ask yourself these questions:

1. What about this will be difficult for me?
2. Do I need/want to do this in order to be married?
3. How can I do this differently, in a way which will make me (us) happy?

So to illustrate:

1. Dress shopping will be lonely and will highlight my lack of family.
2. I do need a dress, and I want to look and feel amazing on my day.
3. I can go shopping with my husband and bridesmaid - the two people who care about me most in the world will support me the best.

Some problems will turn out to be a lot simpler to solve than you originally expected, but others will require a lot of thought, and discussion of different options with your partner.

The important thing to remember here is that it's YOUR wedding. The two of you. Other than the un-changeable legal stuff, there is no right way to get married. I'll talk more later about how to decide exactly what will make your wedding perfect for you, but it's important first that we acknowledge that it isn't all going to be rainbows, butterflies and sugarplums.

Dealing With Loss

One of the most difficult things to deal with on your wedding day is the unavoidable absence of loved-ones who have passed away.

There will be people you wish could be with you, who won't be able to make it. These are things you can't change, and you can't just ignore. You will have your own ways to deal with loss, but by acknowledging that these things are going to be a problem, you can look for ways to honour those you wish were there. You can find ways to make those loved-ones be a part of your day, even in their absence.

There are many ways you can include the departed in your wedding day - from memorial tables and readings in the ceremony, to bouquet brooches and jewellery engravings. It's worth researching these thoroughly to find what will work for you.

TO DIY OR NOT TO DIY?

If you're struggling for budget or time, then DIY can be a help or a hinderance. As with everything else in this process, you need to figure out what's best for you.

How to do it, when you're stressed? Try answering these questions:

1. How much would it cost to get it done professionally?
2. Can I afford it?
3. How much would it cost to DIY?
4. Would I be able to DIY it to a quality level I'll be happy with?
5. Would it be worth the time it takes to DIY?

I'm going to use stationery as an example, as it's the basis of my experience. I'm not going to tell you that you need to pay someone - specifically me - and that you don't have a choice.

In fact, if you want to DIY stationery, that's great!

I love designing and making stationery, it's a really cool hobby that I get to do as a job. I love little fiddly bits of decoration, and I love making sure the tiny details are correct. Honestly, it's my cocaine. And if you like making things, and you find it soothing, then I absolutely encourage you to DIY your invitations. If you've a crafty relative who loves to do it, and they want to help, then go for it.

But sometimes when you've decided to DIY, even with the best will in the world, you just run out of time. So you either hire a professional last minute, which can be expensive, or you buy the first decent, generic ones you see in a supermarket while you do the weekly shop, and then have to spend ages hand-writing all your extra details.

I'm not trying to put you off, honestly, and I'm only using stationery as an example because it's what I know about. So before you commit to DIY or not to DIY, consider the pros and cons, the time investment, and if you will actually enjoy it or not.

GET YOUR DUCKS IN A ROW - WEDDING STATIONERY STYLE

So now we've talked about the problems, how can you start getting all the good stuff in your wedding day? Where do you begin?

Since you became engaged, you've probably had lots of ideas for things you'd like to include in your wedding, Things you've seen on Pinterest, things from other people's weddings you've been to, things you've seen on films or TV.

I'm going to show you the method I like to use with couples who aren't sure where to begin. This is also really useful if you're part way through the process, and have some ideas you're definitely sure of, but a lot of things you're just feeling overwhelmed by.

We're going to run through each of the steps as we go through the book, but the worksheet that follows is a really great way to get all your ideas in one place, so you can easily streamline your planning process, and not waste time on things that neither you nor your partner really want.

I'd recommend you and your partner work together on this. If you're the one doing the bulk of the wedding planning (and if you're reading this book, I'd guess that was the case!) then this is a really great place to get your partner involved. If you can, sit down together for an hour or so with a glass of wine, a cup of tea or a bottle of gin, and work through the sheet together. At this early stage, anything is possible, and there are no bad ideas.

Whatever you decide, the worksheet will help guide you towards finding the style which best suits you both. It can also help make the decisions on where you're best putting your budget to help get the wedding of your dreams.

To download the worksheet, head to:

https://giftast.com/how-to-plan-your-perfect-wedding

and print off a copy. We'll work through each of the headings together over the following pages. I'll give you some ideas of what to think about, and where to look for inspiration.

I'd recommend you read through this whole section first, then prepare to start. So if you're sitting comfortably... Let's begin!

WORKSHEET - DESIGN YOUR WEDDING.

Preparation

We've already mentioned Pinterest as a potential starting point/idea generating machine. If you've not already started looking, then now, right at the beginning of the process, is the best time to start pinning.

If you're new to Pinterest, you can check out our Giftast Pinterest account, as well as our recommendations for some really great boards to follow.

https://uk.pinterest.com/Giftast/

Create a wedding ideas board - you can split this down into different categories, so consider having sections for different colour schemes, various themes you like the idea of, and on-the-day ideas you just love.

Instagram is another great place to go for inspiration. Check out hashtags relating to any vague ideas you might have. If you've no ideas at all, start with hashtags like #weddingplanning and #weddingstyle to get a great overview of what's available.

It may sound like I'm teaching you to suck eggs here, but did I do any of this stuff when I was planning my wedding? No, I did not, and it made everything 10x harder. Keeping a visual record, whether online, in a folder on your desktop, in a notebook, on a mood board or as a collection of magazine cut-outs, gives you your own wedding dictionary to refer back to. If you don't save those images, chances are that you'll forget them, and if you don't pin them when you see them on Pinterest, never expect to see them again :(

Wedding inspiration is everywhere these days, from online, through blogs, to magazines. Don't rush this part - gather everything to you, until you close your eyes and see veils, flowers and cake. Dip in and out of it. Browse while you're catching up on TV, on the bus, or on your lunch break.

Enjoy it - at this point in the process there are no budgets, no impossibilities.

Let yourself play in a universe filled with unicorns, prosecco walls, 50ft dress trains and personalised crockery. And finally, when you feel content with your inspiration collection, leave it for a couple of days. Allow yourself the luxury of time to have it all sink in, so you can return to your ideas with fresh eyes.

Now, we are ready to plan.

Get your partner, print off the worksheets, get a drink and some snacks, and carve out some quality time to talk about your hopes and dreams.

Venue

Not sure of your venue yet? No problem. Write in the area you'd like, and ideas for venues to approach. Church or registry office? If nothing is settled, work with ideas. We can confirm this later, and you don't have to go through the worksheet all in one go.

Date

No date? No worries. Year, season, ideal day… stick it all in. We can finalise it later, but it will help to have an idea at this stage. If you haven't already, now is a great time to have that conversation about exactly when you both envision getting married.

Must Have

This is where all your dancing around in the field of Pinterest dreams starts to pay off. What did you love? What do you absolutely have to have?

Aside from Pinterest, there are likely a couple of weddingy things you really don't want to be without. Be they family heirlooms, reminders of loved ones who can't make it, or a particular flower you've always dreamed of, write them down. You don't want this important stuff to get forgotten among all the wedding-related admin.

Ideas

What are the favourites of the ideas you found from trawling Pinterest/wedding blogs/magazines? What do you want to use as a starting point? What ideas have you had in your head since you became engaged, or even earlier?

This will serve as a quick, written reference point for you to easily look back to. Consider wedding styles, popular themes and photos you'd love to be taken on the day. Be as loose or as specific as you like at this point.

As you're discussing this with your other half, you may decide to shelve some of your ideas, or you may come up with new ones! Write down anything you'd like to explore more.

Time to Get Specific!

We've been working in generalisations so far. However thorough your Pinteresting has been, it's very unlikely that you've covered everything. Use the headings below to note down any thoughts or ideas you and your partner have for each of the below categories. Again, you can be as free-wheeling as you like. We're just making sure all (or rather, as many as possible) bases are covered at this stage.

Wedding Styles

Do you want something formal and black tie? Has a Gatsby-themed party been figuring a lot in your Pins? Perhaps you want something a bit more laid-back and bo-ho. Note down any styles you like and want to consider for your wedding.

Where Did We Meet?

This is a great way to generate ideas you might not otherwise consider. Whether you met at work, at the football, on a skiing holiday or at the gym, take the time to reminisce. Even if it's not something obvious, like locking eyes beneath the Eiffel Tower in Paris, talk about the first few weeks of your relationship.

Was there a song that was the soundtrack to your dating? Is there a special meal you first cooked together? A signature cocktail, a la Wills and Kate, which, now you think about it, you'd like serving at your wedding? Did you go away for a special first holiday together which could inspire you?

There are beautiful memories you can easily overlook, but which can be used to inspire special touches on your wedding day. It's things like this which will make your wedding truly unique and utterly representative of the two of you and your lives together.

Favourite Colours

For my husband and I, we both love burgundy, so we knew that was going to be a big theme in our wedding. Note down both of your favourite colours, and see what could work well together. You could come up with some surprising combinations! It doesn't matter what the Pantone colour of the year is, or what wedding trends are "in". If you love a particular colour, let me reassure you right now, you will be able to find something you can have on your wedding day in that shade.

A great way of doing this is by going down the bespoke stationery route (although I would say that!), because then you're not so seasonally dependant as if you rely on, for example, fresh flowers to carry your theme. And speaking of flowers…

Flowers

What are your favourites? Are there any with special memories for you - any scents you adore? Forget about whether or not they'll be in season for your big day at the moment - remember what we said about using stationery;) and fake flowers are also worth considering, as a much longer lasting keepsake.

Seasonal

Whatever season you've decided to marry in, there will be different things to consider.

In Summer, especially if you've gone for a beach wedding, you might want baskets of flip flops, or blankets for when it gets colder in the evening.

Autumn weddings have the chance of rain, if you're going to be outdoors for photos. Winter could mean sleigh rides, snowmen and Christmas gifts.

If you plan ahead, inconveniences such as rain can become opportunities for stunning pictures, rather than leaving your day a wash-out.

Feeling

Ooh, I love this one. How do you want your wedding to feel? How do you want yourself and your guests to feel? Do you want it casual, with bare feet and a disco? Or do you want something refined, with black tie and ice-sculptures? Do you want to feel super-relaxed on the day, and what can you consider which will help that? Write down some words about how you and your partner make each other feel. What are your favourites, and what do you have in common? You can use this feeling to help whittle down what will and won't work for you on your big day, but we'll get to that later.

Most Important Part Of The Day

What is the most important part of your wedding day? Is it spending the time surrounded by your family and friends? Is it having a certain photo, or commemorating a loved one?

There are no wrong answers here, it's just what works for you.

For me, I wanted a vegan wedding cake. My wedding was the only one I've ever been to, where I could actually eat the cake. And whoo boy, was it a good cake. Two tiers of fudgy, gooey chocolate. Thick white icing - I love icing, but I very rarely get the chance to eat it. It was heaven, and it was one of the first things I arranged. I've still got a picture of that cake, which I look at fondly.

Another important part - I wanted to do a speech. There was no father of the bride to make a speech, but even if there had been, I was sure I wanted a voice on my wedding day. It was really important to me to get that structured into the day, and I did! So think outside the box here - what is most important to you?What Represents You As A Couple, And As Individuals?

Everybody's got a thing. Whether or not you want to make that "thing" part of your wedding is up to you, but it's definitely worth considering in the first instance. If you're crazy about football, then a football-themed seating plan might work for you. Is your cat the most important member of your family? Consider how you can get them involved, from participating in an engagement photoshoot, to having them illustrated on your invitation.

Is The Venue Important?

If you've chosen the venue, then this could be a really big part of your wedding design. From stained-glass inspired stationery if you've gone for a church, to a 20s theme if your venue is Art Deco, you can get loads of inspiration from where your ceremony and reception are going to be held.

If you're getting married in a barn, you might want to consider something more rustic and floral, or you might want to go for something completely different. Remember, there are no right or wrong answers, it's all just about generating ideas. If it's your dream venue, you could have it illustrated on your stationery. Perhaps there are some gorgeous period features you could take inspiration from, and use as a recurring motif. What is it you love about your venue, and how can you use that when designing your day?

Time To Pick Your Favourites!

Now we've rolled around in all our wonderful, glorious off-the-wall ideas, it's time to get more specific. I'd recommend you take some time to think about what you've written down, before you take this next step. More ideas will come to you over the next few days, and you'll want to include them. Now you've fired your imagination up, and got your other half involved, you'll be seeing ideas all over the place! Give yourself a chance to consider them fully.

And when you're finally ready, work through the following categories, grouping together your favourite ideas in whatever way feels right to you.

- Style & Feeling
- Themes
- Must Have
- Colours & Flowers

I use this worksheet with couples who aren't sure what they want their wedding stationery to look like, so the next step would usually be, book in for a free consultation call with me!

https://giftast.com/contact

There's a whole section on stationery at the end of this book – be sure to check that out as well as the rest of my interviews with suppliers, to give you more information on what your options are, and what you'll need to bear in mind when you're planning.

But all that can wait, as we are now ready to talk about my favourite part:

Getting Wedding Sh*t Done

SECTION TWO
Getting it done.

SO NOW YOU KNOW WHAT YOU WANT YOUR WEDDING TO LOOK LIKE - WHAT NEXT?

With your worksheet completed, all your tough decisions have been made for you. Isn't that great? So you're ready - more prepared than ever - to get cracking with making your dream wedding a reality. But - still - there's so much to do! Don't panic - you're further along than you realise.

I'm going to walk you through the six steps which - if you follow them - can help reduce your stress levels around your wedding planning. You may even enjoy it!

The system which follows is the method I developed when working in a high-pressure environment as an Exec PA. This won't work for everyone. And if you don't follow it to the letter, then no problem - but if you try even a little of this, then hopefully it will help.

When your brain is swimming with things you need to do, it can feel overwhelming. You shut down. When you've more to do than your mind can fully process, it feels as though you're trying to grasp the whole universe.

What do I mean? Well, you know space, yeah? The concept of space? I understand that we are on a rock in the middle of a vast expanse of nothingness. I get that we are hurtling through this nothingness at speeds I can't even imagine. But that's it. It's so big and so fast, I can't compare it to anything. None of these things mean anything to mc. It's too much for my brain to fully comprehend.

Like whales - I know they're big, but do I really grasp how big?

No. No I do not.

Whales and space are - to my mind - too big. Like the ocean! I don't like thinking about how big, not to mention, deep, the ocean is. TOO DEEP, to be honest. There are a lot of things of a size so great I can't grasp them. Tempting though it is, I won't list them all here.

And when something is so big I can't even conceive it, that's where my brain stops trying. I have nothing to compare it to. And just like that, if you are overwhelmed by the enormity of the task ahead of you, your brain just... stops.

Which seems like a tangent, I know. But when you're working, and you have this massive to do list and getting all of these things done is your job, you have to find a way through it.

This is my method.

1. Make a big list
2. Decide what's a priority
3. Use a planner
4. Challenge yourself
5. Cut yourself some slack
6. Bask in your own brilliance

That's it - six easy steps. So that's done, book over!

OK, yes, there's more to it than that. I'll go through all of these points in more detail, including some handy hints and tips. We'll talk about how to make real headway and get stuff done.

I'm addicted to crossing things off my to-do list - a day without a to do list is a day where I just don't know what to do with myself. But whether you're a control freak like me, or you just want to dip your toe in as you plan your dream wedding, then these six tips will really help you get there, and with as little stress as possible.

This process falls under the idea of hyperbolic discounting. You can learn more about it on the links at the bottom of the page, from people who are much more qualified to tell you what it actually means than I am. But in short, you're using the brain's preference for making short term, immediate reward decisions to help you actually get things done, rather than procrastinate.

One great thing about this method is that you can use it to get any big jobs done. Writing a book, starting a business, moving house…

So without further ado, let's get started!

HTTPS://MEDIUM.COM/BEHAVIOR-DESIGN/HYPERBOLIC-DISCOUNTING-AEFB7ACEC46E
HTTPS://WWW.ECONOMICSHELP.ORG/BLOG/GLOSSARY/PRESENT-BIAS/

STEP 1 – MAKE A BIG LIST:
GET EVERYTHING DOWN ON PAPER.

Yeah. Sounds obvious. But have you done it? Have you got everything - and I mean everything written down and all in one place for easy access?

You've probably started making lists already. You can't sleep because of things popping into your head. Get it out of your brain and down onto your notebook app, some scrap paper, or in your gorgeous, shiny and new wedding notebook.

I like a spreadsheet for some tasks, (hello, making my Christmas shopping list), or I use Google Docs when I want to add things in to various categories. A good old notebook is my preferred method though, and I find (because I am very into my notebooks) that you have to get the right notebook for you, for the task at hand.

I work using a couple of notebooks at a time - one for personal stuff, writing diaries, plotting stories, working through problems - and one for Giftast - business planning, meeting notes, my big work to do list and so on.

When I start a new notebook, it has to feel really right for the time. This notebook is going to be my companion for anywhere from 3 - 24 months - it has to feel good. It takes me ages to decide what notebook to use, and that's one reason I have oh so many blank notebooks. Because that notebook you saw three years ago in a shop that doesn't exist any more might be the precise notebook you need to use right now.

So take a little time making sure your planned method is one you feel comfortable with. If you're a tactile person, go with paper. If you're glued to your phone, try OneNote. There are also a variety of wedding planning apps you can try.

If you've decided paper is your thing, I'd recommend something A5 - small enough to carry around but not too small to write in comfortably. Grid paper is great for list making. I'd personally avoid using a notebook with plain pages or very closely ruled lines. But hey, it's just whatever makes you comfortable and what feels right for you.

It might sound like I'm going too deep on this. True, it's a personal passion of mine, but this list will be your companion for the entirety of your wedding planning. Not only do you want it to be as easy and natural as possible for you to use, but you deserve a really nice notebook!

So now you've found your dream notebook / spreadsheet / app, we can get into the nitty gritty.

What you want is a master list of everything that needs doing. Then, you need to break it down into small, easily achievable tasks. Simple!

But honestly, I think this is the hardest bit of wedding planning. You're doing a lot of thinking all in one go. What this means is, when you do get some free time to do some wedding admin, you don't have to waste time/get put off by spending 10 minutes deciding what to do. Think how much time that will save you over the course of your entire wedding planning journey! Time you can spend feeling smug and eating chocolate, if you like. (I like).

Where to start?

Where indeed? I always find that I have loads of ideas of things to write on my lists, then as soon as I sit down to write, my mind goes blank. You can get loads of really useful lists online, but to save you the trouble, I've pulled together a quick starting point for you.

You can download a printable copy here:

https://giftast.com/how-to-plan-your-perfect-wedding

STARTER WEDDING TO DO LIST

- ANNOUNCE ENGAGEMENT! ACCEPT CARDS AND CONGRATULATIONS.
- DISCUSS AND SET A WEDDING BUDGET
- COMPLETE DESIGN YOUR PERFECT WEDDING WORKSHEET
- MAKE BIG LIST!
- PLAN WEDDING SIZE
- DRAFT ROUGH GUEST LIST
- DELEGATE TASKS
- SHORTLIST DATES FOR YOUR WEDDING
- SHORTLIST VENUES
- ARRANGE TO VISIT VENUES
- CHOOSE VENUE AND DATE
- CHOOSE STATIONERY
- APPROVE FINAL STATIONERY DESIGNS
- COLLECT ADDRESSES
- SEND SAVE THE DATE CARDS
- RESEARCH LOCAL BRIDAL SHOPS
- ARRANGE DRESS APPOINTMENTS
- CHOOSE MEMBERS OF WEDDING PARTY
    - WITNESSES, BRIDESMAIDS, GROOMSMEN
- RESEARCH AND BUY WEDDING INSURANCE
- RESEARCH AND BOOK PHOTOGRAPHER
- ORDER DRESS!
- RESEARCH & BOOK FLORIST
- RESEARCH AND BOOK HAIR AND MAKE UP ARTIST
- RESEARCH & BOOK CATERER
- RESEARCH AND BOOK TRANSPORT
- FIND CAKE MAKERS
- TASTE CAKES!
- ORDER CAKE
- BOOK HONEYMOON
- SPEAK TO VENUE RE STYLING/CHOOSE EVENTS COMPANY AND BOOK/MAKE DECORATIONS
- BOOK HOTEL ROOMS FOR WEDDING NIGHT
- ARRANGE WEDDING FAVOURS
- SET UP GIFT LIST
- ORDER INVITATIONS

- SEND INVITATIONS
- ARRANGE TO GIVE NOTICE OF MARRIAGE
- BUY GIFTS FOR WEDDING PARTY/EACH OTHER
- ARRANGE DRESS FITTING
- CHOOSE SONGS/READINGS/HYMNS FOR CEREMONY
- COLLECT RSVPS AND FINALISE GUEST LIST
- ORDER ON THE DAY STATIONERY
    - ORDER OF SERVICE
    - TABLE PLAN
    - MENU
    - PLACE CARDS
    - TABLE NUMBERS
- FINALISE WEDDING ACCESSORIES
    - TIES
    - CUFFLINKS
    - JEWELLERY
    - HAIR ACCESSORIES
    - SOMETHING OLD, NEW, BORROWED, BLUE

This isn't an exhaustive list and, depending on how you want your wedding to work, your to-do list might look very different!

But have a good think about every little job which makes up all your big jobs. Think about what you'd be likely to achieve in, say, 15 or 30 minutes.

Having bite-size jobs makes it easier to complete - you're more likely to find 15 minutes than an hour, and can slot your tasks in throughout the day.

So for example, writing invitations could be broken into batches of 25 or 50, and done over the course of several days.

Once you're done, take a look at your undoubtedly massive list. Feel a wave of overwhelm and panic wash over you. Let it pass. Breathe. You got this. Remember - you don't have to do everything yourself. Write initials next to the jobs you can delegate. You know almost everything that needs doing, and you know how long you have.

You have the POWER.

Tips:
- Have a binder/folder for all your wedding stuff, as you'll start collecting paperwork and contracts. It's easy to misplace single sheets of paper, so keep everything in one place.
- Make a new, devoted wedding email address. This way you can just abandon it after your wedding and not have to worry about all those wedding groups you subscribed to.

STEP 2 - DECIDE WHAT IS A PRIORITY
AND MAKE IT NON-NEGOTIABLE.

For me, discovering this was a life-changer. Not as an Exec PA - all my jobs were non-negotiable and had to be done. What I was falling down at was applying this same rule to myself.

It's easy to shrug off the things that make a little difference to your life - and just your life - as unimportant. If you've got kids to look after, pets, or friends and family in need of assistance, it's easy to put your needs to the back of the list.

Self care has become a really big thing recently, and whether you think it's face masks and prosecco, or meditation and tidying up, it's personal to you. Even if you think it's a load of mumbo-jumbo.

Part of looking after yourself is, as far as I'm concerned, taking the time to make things comfortable and easy for yourself, like you do to others. Whether it's making it important that you fill the coffee machine for yourself in the evening before work, or prioritising any small thing which makes you - and only you - benefit.

So, how does this work in wedding planning?

This is what I mean by making something non-negotiable. If you've been putting off phoning a venue because you hate speaking on the phone, or compiling the guest list because you're worried it will cause arguments, you're most likely looking for excuses to put them off, rather than make them happen. And by doing this, you're causing yourself extra stress.

Making something non-negotiable means that, rather than looking for excuses, you're finding ways to make it happen. This is you forcing yourself to look for positive solutions, rather than negative excuses.

When you negotiate with yourself about whether or not you have to, say, go to the gym, you're allowing yourself to have the choice. You don't need to do this to yourself.

If it's not an option to avoid the gym, then you're saving yourself valuable time and energy, and will be feeling better about yourself in the process. Rather than spending all day arguing with yourself about whether you should go or not, you find ways to make it so you have time to do so.

Let me give you an example.

Every day for (at time of writing) a year and 8 months, I have done at least 10 minutes of yoga. I'm not telling you that to brag (much!), but I'm sharing it as an example of what can happen when you make something non-negotiable.

You find the time in your schedule to make it work. I've got up half an hour early to do yoga before I had to go out all day. I've travelled to and from London in a day and got home at 8pm, and done yoga before I ate my dinner so I could crack on with the wine.

I never thought I was the sort of person that could do that, but it's the sort of person I wanted to be.

As soon as something is non-negotiable, you're spending your time thinking about how to make it work, rather than how to get out of it.

So for wedding planning, it might be non-negotiable that you and your partner need to sit down at some point during the week to discuss - and decide - your guest list. Eat the frog, and plan it in so you can open the wine after, or if you get it all done, you can get a takeaway as a reward. But regardless, *it has to be done*.

So go through your list and highlight the big-hitters. What will be best for you to get out of the way early? What are you dreading doing?

As you start to make headway with your to-do list, you'll need to re-visit it, and prioritise new jobs. But start as you mean to go on, and know what you need to get done first.

STEP 3 - PLANNER TIME!

Oh, I love planners. As we've gone through this book together, I think you've got to know me well enough that you could have predicted that.

A couple of years ago, just after we got married, I wanted to start a business. I think we all know what happened with that, and the reason it worked for me was mainly…. Planners.

I hadn't used a planner since my homework diary at school (did everyone have that, or was it just us?) As with most things associated with school, I had no interest in making it part of my life. I was already a big proponent of to-do lists, but they were often vague and disorganised. Jobs like "wedding stationery ideas" and "Think about printers" were often little or no help.

We covered the idea of breaking your jobs down into smaller chunks in Step One, and this is where that hard work pays off. We've decided what's non-negotiable, and now we're going to plan when to do it.

I use a week-to-view diary for my planning. Because I have my master list of little jobs - which I can keep adding to, I don't need to plan for, say, a month, 3 months, or 6 months at a time. I can be a lot more flexible when unexpected things arise.

If you don't want to buy a diary, or it isn't the time of year for it, you can download loads of free, blank, weekly planners, draw one in your notebook in a couple of minutes, stick it on a whiteboard, or whatever you prefer.

Working one week at a time, pick your priorities from your master list, and slot the little jobs into your diary. I'd recommend adding in your day-to-day jobs too, like *clean bathroom*, *buy train season ticket* and *go to Tesco*. You're doing them anyway, and they get you into the habit of crossing things off.

Think about what you've got planned on the week ahead, and schedule things in for when you're most likely to be able to complete them. If you know it'll be a busy week at work, leave things for the weekend.

Take your mood into account too. If, say, you find travelling really draining, don't schedule something in for just after you get back from a long journey. If you menstruate, and it's your time of the month and you know you're going to struggle with certain things as a result of that, don't try to make yourself do them then.

We want to make things as easy as possible for ourselves at this stage. Nobody wants their day to be a hard slog, and it's OK to take your time.

Once a task is completed, just cross it off. I score through with a line so I can still read it, but that's because I like to be able to look back and see the things I've done. It's really useful if you need to remember when you spoke to a supplier, or paid a deposit.

Don't forget to add in things you did that weren't in your planner - and immediately cross them off!

I like to do my planning on a Sunday - and so I write *plan for next week* on every Sunday.

You will also have the satisfaction of crossing things you did in the previous week off your master list, when you're planning the next.

48

Sometimes, if I'm not sure how a job will turn out, or I'm not sure of what I've got on all week, I'll only plan for a couple of days at a time, rather than the full week. It's about making it work for you, and allowing yourself some flexibility. If, for example, you don't know how much of a task you'll be able to get done, you're giving yourself some leeway to take some extra time if you need it, without throwing your schedule out of whack.

I like to go easy on what I put in my planner on weekends. This means I can add in more if I've got time, go back to things I didn't get to, or I can use my free time to do other tasks and get ahead of myself.

But then again, I am a planner addict whose only idea of fun is strictly organised fun. As you start using a planner, you'll figure out what does and doesn't work for you.

STEP 4 - CHALLENGE YOURSELF

This one comes with a warning.

Once you've started, you might be surprised by how much you can get done. By making your master list, the most difficult part is over. You've made things easy for yourself by scheduling things based on when you're most likely to be in the mood to do them.

Thinking about what you need to do can take longer than actually doing one or two of your little jobs. You can crack a couple of these out in a lunch break, if you've planned ahead.

Crossing things off your to do list - and feeling that little thrill of accomplishment is addictive.

If one wedding task a day is working out, maybe knock it up to two some days! If you've a busier day coming up but you still want to feel like you're making progress, find one of the more fun or quick tasks (e.g. looking at Instagram for inspo/texting your third cousin for her address) and pop it in on that day.

But here's the warning:

Don't push yourself too far.

If you're overloading your day, and you can't get to everything, it can be really disheartening. Yes, challenge yourself to cross one more thing off your list while you're waiting in for the plumber or stuck on a delayed train. But schedule realistically. It's the classic "under promise, over deliver". And you can use that on yourself, too.

Remember - we're trying to make things less stressful, so don't heap jobs on yourself, as that will cause you unnecessary stress. It's incredible how fast things can get done sometimes, but those times are sprints. Just like Usain Bolt can't run at top speed for more than 100 metres, you need to walk, jog, and sprint, and sometimes, come to a complete stop.

Which brings us to...

STEP 5 - CUT YOURSELF SOME SLACK

This is a brief section, but don't let that fool you into thinking it's unimportant. As a self-confessed planner-aholic, the act of actually stopping and allowing myself to rest is something I really struggle with. Running my own business and working from home means that the lines between rest and work are so blurred that I sometimes struggle to remember what I actually do to relax any more. Let me be a cautionary tale, and set out early on to find the balance that works for you.

One of the main focuses of this guide is, I hope, to help you balance this sudden influx of extra wedding admin on top of your other commitments and *normal life* in a way that doesn't stress you out. But getting things done can feel like a super power, and the addictive pleasure of crossing things off a to-do list can be difficult to give up.

Unexpected things happen. Sometimes you have a bad day, there's a traffic jam, you just need to sleep. Other people need your time, you have to work late, or what you thought was a little job turns into a big one.

Don't stress. You got this, remember?

That's the beauty of working through these little, little jobs, and only planning up to a week at a time. You can cross it off another day. Or you can push it back to next week. Maybe you can give it to someone else to do. The important thing is that you're in control of everything that needs doing, and you can move things around. You know what's non-negotiable and what there's some flexibility with.

Because you have an overview of everything you need to do, you are always in control.

The difficulty can lie in allowing yourself to be flexible.

There are days - and weeks - where the best thing for me has been to ignore my planner, or not plan at all. If it's all too much, give yourself a break. You deserve it. Planning a wedding should be fun.

You are allowed to go at your own pace.

If the stress is mounting, and you're feeling overwhelmed by the sheer volume of little things you need to do, then here is my advice.

Step back. Ask yourself - ***do I really need this?***

I'm not talking about the big stuff, I'm talking about the minutiae. Whenever you're planning something big, you find yourself sweating the small stuff. But consider - when you're looking back on your big day, is it something you'll care about?

Getting swept up in all of the details is easy to do, and yes - perhaps you'll notice if the ribbon on your flowers is two shades darker than the bridesmaids dresses. But perhaps you won't. Perhaps nobody will.

If it's important to you, then by all means worry about it. But if it's stressing you out then consider if it's worth the cost.

And here's another thing - plan in some fun.

Yes, I love organised fun, but that's not precisely what I mean here. Plan doing nice things. Schedule in a long bath for yourself, or to read a couple of chapters of a romance novel. Plan in some time with your partner where you don't talk about the wedding, perhaps over a romantic dinner. Be nice to yourself. Make doing the nice things non-negotiable.

Time of the Month

If you menstruate, then that's worth bearing in mind too. There will be times of the month where you naturally have more energy than others, and planning in making a whole heap of phone calls or trips to venues when you want nothing more than to curl up in a tiny ball and watch Netflix is doing yourself an unkindness. Not only will you resent every moment of these tasks you just don't want to do, but you'll not be in a frame of mind to make good choices. Listen to yourself, and set yourself up to succeed.

Getting to know your cycle and working with it instead of against it is something I cannot recommend highly enough. If this is something that interests you, check out Maisie Hill's incredible book, Period Power. It's a bona fide life changer.
So now we've mastered our to do list, prioritised, scheduled, challenged ourselves and made time to relax. What next?

STEP 6 - BASK IN YOUR OWN BRILLIANCE

As you work through your week, and then go back to your master list, you're going to start to be pleasantly surprised by how much you've got done. Suddenly, big jobs are completed and you barely broke a sweat.

And you should be so proud. Regardless of how you do it, planning a wedding is a big job, and a lot of work. Even if you're paying someone to do the planning for you, it can still be a stressful experience. But you're doing it, and hopefully having fun along the way.

Stress is an awful thing to be caught up in, and it has a multitude of bad effects on our health[1]. Modern life on its own can be hugely stressful to both our bodies and our minds. It shouldn't be the case that the happiest day of your life should take such a toll on you in the run up. So find what works for you, dial down the stress, and enjoy the process.

Using a planner and crossing things off works best for me because I can look back at a week and see everything I achieved. There's no way I can remember everything I've done each day, but when I look back at what I've crossed out, I'm genuinely always surprised by how much I've done. And when I'm crossing things off my master to-do list, I'm really proud of myself.

We work really hard, whether at work, looking after family/kids/pets, or planning a wedding. We deserve to give ourselves the credit for our hard work and we deserve to put the effort in to make things easier for ourselves.

If this method has worked for your wedding planning, consider if it could help you with any other aspects of your life. If you spend that time at the beginning of the week breaking tasks down and planning ahead, you're taking a lot of the effort out of actually doing them.

1 https://www.nhs.uk/conditions/stress-anxiety-depression/understanding-stress/

I do find that putting something in the planner means it has a higher chance of getting done. Little things I'd otherwise forget, like *take dinner out of the freezer*, *brush the cat* or *soak beans for tomorrow's tea*. They all get done because I don't even have to think about it.

I just look in my planner.

So them's the tips. I know it's not for everyone, but I really hope it helps. The most important thing I can suggest is writing that big list. Seeing exactly what needs doing, physically in front of you, gives you so much more control over what you can get done and how and when you do it. It means you are running the wedding planning; it's not controlling your life.

SECTION THREE

Resources

INTERVIEWS WITH SUPPLIERS:

I've chatted with some of my favourite wedding suppliers to give you the lowdown on what you should be looking for, what questions to ask, and what you'll need to plan for.

I'm going to start with stationery, which isn't an interview, because how unbearably pretentious would I have to be to pretend to interview myself?

Stationery

Perhaps your invitations, table plans and thank you cards aren't something you've given much thought to, but by starting with a strong idea of how you want your wedding to look and feel, you can carry this theme from Save The Dates all the way through the big day itself and on to Thank you cards and anniversary gifts.

Off The Shelf

There are loads of great options for budget-friendly wedding stationery available nowadays. We offer a budget range at Giftast, and there are loads of gorgeous ranges available on the high street and cheaply online.

This can be really handy if you've got a broad theme, or if you're on a tight budget. The downside is that it does limit you on what you can include - you might struggle for matching info cards, for example, and you'll have a lot of hand-writing to do to include all your wedding details.

Range Stationery

I'm putting this in a separate category from Off The Shelf, as here I'm talking about stationery from a wedding stationer. This is stationery that is already designed, but which can be personalised to include your own details. At Giftast, we will change our range items to fit your colour scheme for no extra charge ;)

Range stationery items from a wedding stationer are a lot more flexible when it comes to personalising. For example, you'll be able to get any extras you want to include - like info cards - printed to match the rest of your stationery, and if you want a matching sign for the sweet cart and the flip flop basket - well, that's something we can help with too. Other suppliers may vary, but generally, when you're working directly with a stationer, there will be plenty of flexibility on their range designs, although the costs of that may vary.

Bespoke Stationery

Put simply, bespoke stationery is when a design is created just for you, to your specifications. Whether you've a strong vision of exactly what you want, or you just know that you want something really personal, bespoke stationery can tick all your boxes. It can seem daunting if you've never worked with an artist before, but with your worksheet completed and your ideas firmed up, you're in a great position to streamline the design process, and get a strong design you absolutely love.

I'm not going to lie to you - I love bespoke. I love working with couples to create a design which really captures them. The really great thing about bespoke is that it's entirely yours - and you can do whatever you want with it.

We're in the age of Instagram, where you are your own brand.

We can use bespoke wedding stationery to create a "logo" for you and your partner - something which represents you both as individuals as well as a couple, and can be used to create wonderful keepsakes throughout your lives together.

Wedding stationery is a relatively inexpensive way to make your wedding "Brand You" - compared to the cost of the venue or the dress, for example, it can have some of the biggest impact at the lowest price.

What Wedding Stationery Do I Need?

I think there's this pressure of what you *have to have* for your wedding, and if you Google something like "What Wedding Stationery Do I Need?", then you'll see an enormous and expensive-sounding list of everything you could possibly think of. It can often feel like too much.

Of course, not everyone will feel this wedding-related peer pressure, but if budget is an issue, it can be difficult to decide what can be cut.

So let's talk about what you might actually need, as well as a couple of options which are nice to have, if they suit your purpose.

Save The Dates

Do I need them?

Not necessarily.

Do I want them?

Perhaps. If you're planning a wedding for, say, 2 years away, then Save The Dates are a brilliant idea. Particularly paper ones - they'll get stuck on a notice board, so when your most important guests are planning their holidays, they can just look at it. No rooting in emails, or scrolling back through text messages. Definitely worth considering, but if you're only planning for under a year away? Maybe not worth it.

Invitations

Do I need them?

Yeah, pretty much. Unless you're eloping

Do they have to be paper?

No. But again, the stick-em-on-the-noticeboard thing. And I would say that, of course!

Your invitations can be as simple or as complicated as you like. If you want to go all out with a beautifully crafted pack, then that's a gorgeous keepsake your guests can treasure. If you want to buy a multi pack of cards you fill out yourself, that's your choice. DIYing your own can be a great option if you're a creative person.

Information Cards

Do I need them?

Maybe. If your venue is out of the way, or not local to most of your guests, an info card with recommended hotels and taxi numbers could be really useful, and save you from having to answer a lot of Facebook messages! You can also add on your gift preferences, dress code, or any other pertinent information.

What are my options?

Well, if we're talking paper, you've got 3 main choices:

1. Double sided invitations - if you've space, stick it on the back! Here at Giftast we do that for no extra cost.

2. Add a separate info card - if your invitations have a back design already (we do quite a few with monograms) then you can add in another card, almost identical, but with your extra info. This will cost more, though.

3. Add it in to a folded card - for folded invites, extra info can be added in to the front left inside page. We also do this for no extra cost, and it has the added benefit of keeping all your information together.

RSVPs

Do I need them?

Perhaps, but maybe not.

What are my options?

Paper RSVPs are really nice, I think, because they're so smol[1]. Ours are A7, so half the size of a standard postcard, and come with matching sized return envelopes. When they get posted back to you, they're adorable. It's so nice receiving fun post, and it's a physical reminder of the excitement and build up to your wedding as they are slowly returned to you.

[1]HTTPS://WWW.DICTIONARY.COM/E/SLANG/SMOL/

But if you don't care about smol cute post, why bother? Well, if you've a lot of technologically un-advanced guests coming, it may be easiest for them the reply by snail mail. But if you're on a tight schedule, or everyone you're inviting loves to text or email, then you could just add those RSVP details on to your invitation/info card and save yourself the trouble.

It's your wedding, it's your budget, and there's no one-size-fits all for wedding stationery. Have a chat to your stationer about what you actually want, and what will work best for you.

I'll tackle the mind-boggling array of On-The-Day stationery later, but for now, let's look in more detail about what you may wish to include on your stationery.

What To Include On Save The Dates

The Date

It sounds obvious, but you will need to know the exact date of your wedding. You will almost certainly need to have booked your venue before you send these out. If your wedding isn't on a weekend, it may be helpful to include the day in addition to the date. Timings aren't necessary on a Save the Date, and you may only be finalising these nearer the time.

Your Names

Again, sounds obvious, but sometimes it's the most obvious things which get forgotten when you're stressed! It's your choice as to whether or not you include your surnames.

Note That An Invitation Will Follow

Just to avoid confusion for your guests! Your Save the Date is necessarily brief, and as it's sent well in advance of the big day, you can't include much information because you won't know it yet!

Optional - Their Names

If you're sending the Save the Date to an address where some residents are invited and some aren't, you may wish to include names to avoid disappointment and arguments later. Our personalised Save the Dates can include either a line for you to write in the names of your guests, or be printed with individual names. Otherwise, you can just include names on the envelope and confirm with the invitation which follows.

Optional - Location

If your wedding is taking place in a different country, or somewhere difficult to get to, it can be nice to include a location. Your guests may need to save dates around the big day for travelling.

Optional - Anything else you want.

Remember, there are no hard and fast rules. This is your wedding, and all the above is only a suggestion. There is a lot of tradition around what is sent when, and what information needs to be included. This may not always be relevant to you and your wedding. The most important thing is that it works for you.

Your Wedding, Your Rules!

What To Include On Invitations

Date

Including Day, Month and Year. It's better to be as specific as possible!

Time

It's worth considering including time of ceremony, time of reception, and time of "carriages". This information will also be different depending on whether you're doing separate day and evening invites.

Location (Ceremony & Reception)

Let your day guests know if they need to anticipate travelling between venues. Again, the information provided may be different depending on if you're sending out separate day and evening invitations.

RSVP Details

Are you including a card, or asking people to reply by text/email? When do they need to let you know by?

Plus One

Who is invited? Are your single friends allowed to bring their current SO? Can the kids come? Specify now, to save awkward questions later, and from making your table plan more complicated than it needs to be!

Also worth considering...

Dress Code/Theme

Want everyone to wear purple? Going for a chilled out, shorts and sandals vibe? Going Gatsby? Now's the time to let your guests know, so they can begin planning their outfits.

Gift Requests

Whether you have a gift registry set up, or want money for your honeymoon, or even nothing at all, let your guests know your plans.

Wedding Website

If you've too much information to include on your invitation and don't want to include a separate information card, then you might want to consider making a wedding website, and including the web address on your invitations.

Taxi Numbers

Your more organised guests will bring the invitation on the wedding day, so they will have all the timing and location information to hand. Including taxi numbers is especially useful in areas with limited internet access.

Recommended Local Hotels

Encourage forward planning and cut down on how many phone calls you get all asking the same question - include your recommendations for hotels, including any information regarding reserved rooms at your venue, if necessary.

Directions

Whether your guests are arriving by plane, train, or automobile, and even though a lot of people will just use Google maps, save your guests some time by including some directions to harder-to-find and more out of the way venues. A lot of venues will have this information on their websites.

And then... anything you like! Every wedding is different and you need to think about what works for you. When DH and I got married, we had a morning ceremony, followed by a wedding buffet which we then left at 3pm to go on honeymoon. We included this information on our invites, to let the guests know what to expect, but also so they knew that the venue was still available for their use once we'd left.

All I would say is, the more information you include, the less questions you'll have to answer and the more time you'll save!

What To Include On RSVPs

Guest Names

You can include a space for your guests to write their names, their plus ones, their kids.... You may also want to include a space for number of guests, which could be helpful when pulling together your seating plan!

Accepting / Declining

This can be a general yay/nay depending on which portion of the day you've sent the guest an invitation to. Or, get specific with a day/evening tick box.

Special Dietary Requirements

Super helpful! Avoid any nasty allergies ruining your guests' day, and get this information right at the start of your menu-planning process.

Optional Extras...

- Song Choice - to get your guests dancing at the reception!

- Meal Choice - handy if you've sent out menu options with your invitation.

- Accommodation required?

- Advice for the happy couple.

Remember, it's your special ceremony, so add a request for any information which will make your planning easier and less stressful!

What On The Day Wedding Stationery Do I Need?

There are so many options for on-the-day that it can seem overwhelming. But again, it's a matter of pick and mix - you may want some, and you may want none!

Order of Service

Do I Need It? Maybe.

This one probably depends most on the type of ceremony you're having. If you're including a lot of personal readings, it can be nice to include these on your order of service. That makes this a really nice keepsake both for your guests and yourselves. You can also use your order of service to let guests know the timings for the rest of the day.

Table Plan

Do I Need It? Probably.

For my own wedding, a very small affair, and mostly including DH's family/friends rather than mine, we decided against a table plan, however we are the only people I've heard of doing it that way!

This worked for us because we had

> a) 40 guests who mostly knew one another already, and

> b) a serve-yourself buffet meal.

I made a poster explaining that guests could pick their place cards up at the door (copper plant markers with their names on) and stick them in the table centres (decorated herb pots) on the tables of their choice. This probably won't work for larger parties, and is unlikely to work for sit-down meals, but it's worth noting that other options are available.

Table Numbers

Do I Need Them? Almost Certainly!

If you've opted for a Table Plan then you almost definitely need table numbers/names. But do they need to be printed? Not necessarily - this can be an opportunity to get creative with your table centres, and merge the two.

Place Cards

Do I Need Them? Probably.

Unless you're going all out on a scenario similar to my wedding breakfast, you're going to need to do place cards. If your budget can stretch to it, I'd recommend getting your guest names printed on (at Giftast we always include a few blank spares for those last-minute changes). However, if your budget is tighter, either buy blank to write yourself, or consider ideas for combining place cards with wedding favours. There are loads of ideas for how to do this on Pinterest.

Menus

Do I Need Them? Perhaps, but probably not.

Some people like their guests to know what they're eating, some don't mind.

If your guests have picked their menu choices, this can be better added on to the inside of their place cards, as most people will have no recollection of what they asked for months/over a year earlier! If you're serving everyone the same, a menu can be a nice touch, and also an opportunity to include some more handy information. For example:

- Timings for the rest of the day

- Special thanks

- Information re any donations you did in lieu of wedding favours

- Taxi phone numbers for later in the night.

Signs

Do I Need Them? Well, it depends on what information you want to communicate to your guests.

Are you having:

- flip flops,

- blanket baskets,

- photo booth,

- wedding hashtags,

- Please-don't-post-on-Facebook-yet instructions,

- welcome messages,

- sweet stations,

- reserved seats....

If so, then a sign can be a really nice way of flagging these up to your guests. But most people know a sweet station when they see it, so just go with what feels right for you! At Giftast, if you order table numbers, we will make matching signs the same size and shape for the same price (£2 ish each). But talk to your stationer, as you can also have posters, chalk boards, standing banners, table-plan sized boards...

And there you have it! A non-conclusive list of things you can have - but don't necessarily need.

VENUE

CROWNE PLAZA®
HOTELS & RESORTS
AN **IHG**® HOTEL

Harriet Brace
Meetings and Events Coordinator
Crowne Plaza, Leeds.

Hotel number: 0871 942 9170
Email: events@cpleeds.com
Website: www.cpleedshotel.co.uk/weddings

Facebook: Crowne Plaza Leeds
Instagram: crowneplazaleeds
Twitter: CrownePlazaLDS

Hi, my name's Harriet and I am the Wedding Coordinator at Crowne Plaza Hotel Leeds and I have been at the hotel for two years. Throughout this time I have provided a dedicated and personalised service to couples throughout their planning journey to achieve the wedding of their dreams! Our hotel is passionate about Yorkshire in its entirety – its food, the warmth and friendliness of the people of God's Own Country plays a prominent part in both our wedding packages and the service we provide.

My role as Wedding Coordinator is to liaise directly with couples, from point of enquiry right the way through to the Big Day, guiding them through the planning stages and offering experience and advice throughout. I have the most up-to-date event trends at my fingertips to help each couple design a wedding that best reflects their style and personality, working with our incredible recommended suppliers. I am also here to reassure those pre-wedding nerves! I work closely with the Wedding Host too, who runs the day with precision and detail, allowing every couple to thoroughly enjoy themselves knowing that everything is fully taken care of.

We're ready to help our couples create a wedding day that combines luxury and glamour with affordability, with our all-inclusive wedding packages. Feel free to get in touch - we look forward to hearing from you!

Photo by Richard Wilson – www.richardwilsonphotography.co.uk

What are your top 3 tips for choosing the perfect venue?

When booking a venue, make sure that it is the right venue for you as a couple and not just to wow your guests. It is your special day!

Try and envisage your wedding at the venue. Make the most of attending wedding fairs and showcase events, or try to arrange evening appointments the night prior to a wedding to view the rooms fully set.

If the venue is perfect, but the wedding package isn't quite to your *taste just ask! Most venues, including ours, would be more than happy to look to tailor the package wherever possible.*

What's your number 1 piece of advice for a stress-free wedding day?

Don't underestimate the importance of a wedding planner book or notepad! It is the perfect place to keep all contact details for suppliers, a list of any decorations, photography packages, menus, upcoming appointments and when payments are due. Keep this by your bed or in your handbag for any other details and thoughts!

Photo by Richard Perry - www.richardperryphotography.com

What don't people normally know about your job that you wish they did?

Planning a wedding doesn't stop with the Wedding Coordinator – it is an entire venue operation. At the hotel we liaise with all departments, including Food and Beverage, Operations and Front Office teams to ensure that the day runs smoothly and no detail is missed. There's a lot of preparation and organisation done behind the scenes.

What info do couples need to know when they're looking to book a venue?

At the beginning of the journey, the couple will not have a lot of detailed information. It is helpful though if they have an idea of where the ceremony will take place (is this at the same wedding venue or will the couple and guests be travelling from elsewhere?), the number of daytime and evening guests including children, and what month and year is being considered for their big day.

What should couples bear in mind when picking a venue?

There is a lot to consider when picking the ideal venue!

o *Style – does the venue suit the couple's style? It is so important for them to feel comfortable and that the venue reflects their taste in décor and food.*

o *Venue staff – this is so important! The attentiveness and attitude of staff right from the first show round will give you an idea of how your wedding journey will be.*

o *Location – how are the couple and their guests going to travel to the venue and is any overnight accommodation required?*

o *Budget – the venue is just one element of the day, so keep this in mind when signing the contract!*

How far in advance should couples be booking a venue?

You can book a wedding as soon as you are ready, so long that the venue is taking bookings that far ahead, and have the date available. Two years in advance is plenty of time to enjoy your planning journey.

PHOTOGRAPHER

Hannah Larkin
PHOTOGRAPHY

www.hannahlarkinphotography.com
www.facebook.com/hannahlarkinphotography
www.instagram.com/hannahlarkinphotography
www.twitter.com/hannahlarkin

Hannah Larkin Photography – Wedding photographer London and beyond

I'm Hannah – I'm a wedding and family photographer with a relaxed, natural style that focuses on capturing emotions and telling the story of your day. I live in London, have a base in Northumberland and travel across the UK and overseas photographing weddings from intimate elopements to multi-day wedding celebrations with hundreds of guests.

I first got a camera when I was 7 years old to share views and adventures with my mum who was unwell, and I really fell in love with photography travelling the world from the Arctic to the Antarctic and lots in between. I have a background in psychology so I naturally focus on emotions, and I've now been photographing weddings for over five years. My own multi-cultural wedding celebrations in the UK and Malaysia showed me how it's possible to include traditions, cultures, families and personalities in a wedding – and I always look for ways my couples have personalised their day.

I'm a listener, an observer, a traveller and psychologist. I love to understand people, to find out what matters to them and what makes them tick. I care about getting to know my clients and feel lucky that many become friends. I'm often told how calming I am, and helping you relax is important to me as it allows me to capture authentic moments when you're truly yourself. I look for small, secret signs of love – a glance, a gesture – and personal touches that tell your story and show what makes you unique.

Photo by Hannah Larkin - www.hannahlarkinphotography.com

What are your top 3 tips for getting the wedding photos of your dreams?

1) Have a prewed or engagement shoot. I can't recommend this highly enough. It gives you a chance to get used to being photographed, and to feel relaxed in front of the camera. It lets your photographer get used to working with you, and lets you and your photographer get to know each other. It gets over any awkwardness or shyness, and allows you to have more relaxed and natural wedding portraits.

2) Let your photographer know what's important to you. If you've made your own wedding cake, or a friend has written a table plan for you, if you've spent hours finding the perfect bunting or half your wedding budget on your shoes – let your photographer know. I always aim to capture all the details on your wedding day, but I will pay extra attention to those I know mean the most to you.

3) Do your day your way. Whether that's having your grandma as your maid of honour or including pets in your wedding, having a civil, celebrant-led or religious ceremony, and having as few or as many guests as feels right for you. You might want your wedding day to include time to jump in a river or go on safari, to fill your reception with board games, books or a silent disco, you might choose a garden, glasshouse or woodland wedding, or opt for yurts & tipis, a farm, country house or hotel. If you celebrate the way you want, you'll find that joy and happiness will shine out of you and be visible in your photos.

Oh, and my extra bonus tip – breathe! It's amazing how many people hold their breath when they have their photo taken, and just taking a breath makes your photos look instantly more relaxed and natural.

Number 1 piece of advice for a stress-free wedding day?

Planning. This is my top tip for a stress-free wedding day. I'm a big planner – I love lists and spreadsheets and will always talk through a wedding day timeline with my couples. If you want group photos, I'll ask you to think about them in advance and make sure we have a list of names so I can easily check them off and ensure this part of the wedding runs as smoothly as possible, leaving you time to enjoy your reception. I always google the sunset time for a wedding date and location in the UK depending on your venue & wedding date, sunset can vary from 3.30pm to 10pm - so I recommend that you plan to make the most of the natural light and catch some beautiful golden light in the hour before sunset. Make a plan for bad weather too – for UK weddings at least you can never guarantee it will be dry, so make sure you have an indoor backup option.

If you've got to know your photographer, built trust through an engagement shoot, communicated and planned with them so there's time available for portraits, and you've delegated as much as possible (to a wedding coordinator, planner or your wedding party) then you can relax. This lets you savour the moment - breathe, smell your flowers, look at your new husband or wife – and this will show in gorgeously natural & relaxed wedding photos.

Photo by Hannah Larkin - www.hannahlarkinphotography.com

What don't people normally know about your job that you wish they did?

There are two things I wish people knew about my job...

1) That I travel. People often look only at photographers local to their wedding venue, but I (and many other photographers) happily travel across the UK and overseas. So, I'd advise you to find a photographer whose style you love, who you connect with and like, and talk to them about them travelling to you.

2) That you're not just paying for the hours on the day. Wedding photography prices generally include all the planning and preparation (I talk to my couples about their timeline, do an engagement shoot, get to know them and research their venue) and also lots of work after the wedding (selecting shots, editing, and presenting images). Make sure you check in advance what's included in the price – depending on the photographer this may include some or all of the following: an online gallery, hi res digital files, album, prints and slideshows.

Photo by Hannah Larkin - www.hannahlarkinphotography.com

What info do couples need to know when they're looking to book a photographer?

If you have your heart set on a certain photographer, get in touch with them first, before you book your venue, so you can ensure they're available on your date. Otherwise, let your photographer know the date, ceremony time and venue and give them a little idea about the wedding – is it a relaxed garden wedding or an intimate city elopement, a festival style wedding in a tipi, or a luxurious wedding in a country house. Also, think through what you'd like – do you want all the edited digital files so you can print and use them as you wish, an online gallery to share images with family and friends overseas, a printed keepsake wedding album, or a wedding slideshow to tell the story of your day?

What should couples bear in mind when picking a photographer to work with?

There are a lot of wedding photographers to choose from – I'd recommend using the following four steps to find the right photographer for you.

1) Approach. There are different approaches to wedding photography from 'Reportage' (a paparazzi or documentary approach) to 'Dramatic' (a highly posed or staged approach). In between the two you'll find 'Lifestyle' photography (my approach) which aims for a sense of 'you on a good day' – so unlike reportage approaches I will look for pretty backdrops and give you gentle prompts to help you into relaxed poses, but unlike dramatic approaches I don't often use external lights or spend lots of time setting up a specific shot.

2) Style. Separate to approach, there are different wedding photography styles. These range from moody darker images with lots of shadows, to very light white images, and between these two are colourful images. I'm a natural light photographer and my style tends towards lighter rather than darker images but with a love of capturing the colours you've chosen for your day.

3) Personality & skills. Photographers are all different! You'll end up spending a large portion of your wedding day with your photographer, so it's important to find someone you like and feel comfortable with. Depending on your day you may also want your photographer to have specific skills – sadly I can't dive so I'm no good for underwater weddings – that's the only sort of wedding I say no to as I love working with people of any age, religion, ethnicity or sexuality. My skill set means I'm super organised, I love children and animals, and my psychology background means I focus on emotions as well as being really good at keeping you calm and relaxed.

4) Budget. I know wedding budgets are tricky to manage, but I'd encourage you to allocate a good portion of your budget to your photography. Your wedding photographs are one of the few tangible things you have as a keepsake of your wedding. You want to be filled with happiness and taken right back to that day every time you look at them, to share them with everyone who was there and everyone who couldn't be. You want a visual story of your wedding to be treasured all your life and for generations to come – letting you relive the day, seeing the emotions of those around you, bringing back memories and sharing moments you missed.

And remember you don't need to be limited to photographers in your local area, as most wedding photographers are happy to travel across the UK and overseas.

Photo by Hannah Larkin - www.hannahlarkinphotography.com

How far in advance should couples be booking their photographer?

You should book your photographer as soon as you can, if you have your heart set on a certain photographer – popular dates can book up 2 years in advance, but if you are having a shorter engagement, or you've left things to the last minute it's still worth asking as there is often some space for last minute bookings. I take on only a small number of weddings each year so I can dedicate time to get to know my couples, to talk about their plans and understand what's important to them so I can create photos that truly tell their story.

FLOWERS

H ∧ R E + H ☾ W L

—— F L O R I S T R Y ——

t: 07821 653725
e: elichia@hareandhowl.co.uk
https://www.facebook.com/hareandhowlfloristry/
https://www.instagram.com/hareandhowl/

Hare and Howl Floristry is a wedding floristry company established in the summer of 2018 and is run from our studio in central York, North Yorkshire. We provide bespoke floral designs for weddings and events, striving to create an experience that goes above and beyond your expectations. We aim to create a sense of theatre in our designs; focusing on nature, nostalgia and the curiosity of life.

We aim to bring floristry in line with modern business, offering a range of options which can scale to your needs at a time and cost to suit. Our commitments to affordability, agility and sustainability are what differentiates us from "just another florist", ensuring that all our commissions are given the care and commitment they deserve.

What are your top 3 tips for choosing the perfect wedding flowers?

Stay true to your own style. Remember, a wedding is a day to celebrate the union of two people in love, and your wedding styling should reflect that by showcasing both of your personalities. Whether you are lovers of the latest trends, influenced by the seasons or prefer to keep it elegant and classic, try to communicate a little bit about who you are and what you like to your florist, and they will be able to work with you and create wedding flowers that truly reflect you as a couple.

Create a budget for your flowers, along with wish list of all the floral requirements for the wedding. My experience as a wedding florist has taught me couples tend to underestimate the cost of wedding flowers, therefore when you begin talking to your florist, be upfront about your budget and your floral needs. Decide what are your must have items i.e. bridal bouquet, buttonholes, centrepieces, ceremony flowers, and then see if there is any room left for the remaining decorations such as cake table flowers, thank you bouquets, floral archways etc. If the budget doesn't allow for everything on the list I would much rather create fabulous floral pieces for the essentials that are show stopping and beautiful than stretch the budget out as thinly as possible to create lots of budget arrangements.

Keep an open mind. There are so many flower and foliage varieties out there to create stunning floral designs, seasonality may also play a role in your flower choices. Do some research; Instagram and Pinterest are amazing sources for ideas and inspiration. Also chat with your florist, they should be able to inspire you with out of the ordinary floral choices.

Number 1 piece of advice for a stress-free wedding day?

On the day, wedding coordination is something that I would recommend. An experienced and proficient wedding coordinator should be able to liaise with suppliers and vendors, the venue itself, keep the wedding party and guests organised and to schedule ensuring the day goes without a hitch. And if there are any issues to sort out they won't fall on your lap to sort, they may well be rectified *before you are even aware of anything being amiss.*

What don't people normally know about your job that you wish they did?

When you hire a wedding florist, you are hiring a complete service and not just paying for the final products. A wedding florist brings experience, expertise and design knowledge. From start to finish we spend time communicating and meeting with couples, planning and creating proposals, designing, researching, sourcing the highest quality products, visiting your venue, sometimes coordinating with your other suppliers, buying the flowers at the correct time and conditioning them so they look their best for the wedding day. Depending on the scale of the wedding, there may be several days worth of creating arrangements, onsite setup the day before, delivery on the morning of the wedding, set up for the ceremony and reception, returning the next day to pick up hired vases/arches etc., disposing of flowers if not being kept, cleaning all hired items and packing away back to storage.

What info do couples need to know when they're looking to book a florist?

For me, when a couple gets in touch to discuss flowers for their wedding the most important things are –

- *Date of wedding*
- *Venue*
- *Budget for flowers*
- *A rough idea of numbers of arrangements required i.e. number of centrepieces, bridesmaids, buttonholes etc.*

What should couples bear in mind when picking a florist to work with?

When choosing a wedding florist, look for a florist whose style and brand you relate to. Do your research, look at their previous work, read their "about me" on their website and book a consultation to meet them in person, this often gives you a gut instinct whether they are the right fit for your wedding. Remember there are also different budgets to consider, some florists don't have a minimum spend whereas others have a minimum spend of £1500 for example.

How far in advance should couples be booking a florist?

Booking your florist as soon as possible to ensure you secure your date is always the best advice, I would say generally for the peak wedding season dates of June through to September at least 12 months in advance is normal. However, bookings are taken anywhere from 18 months upwards in some cases, so if you have a particular florist you would love to work with get in touch as soon as you can.

DRESSES

www.bridalreloved.co.uk
T: 01904 331541
M: 07939 193227
E:
york@bridalreloved.co.uk
Instagram:
/bridalrelovedyork/
Twitter @bridalrelovedyo

My name is Elizabeth Matfin and I am the owner of Bridal Reloved in York. I am passionate about all things wedding, and as you'd expect, I absolutely love wedding dresses! I love meeting brides and their friends and family to help them find their perfect dress.

I have lots of fun sourcing the dresses I stock and want my boutique to be a place full of wonderful "finds". I love quirky unusual dresses, vintage style and gothic as well as classic elegant styles.

I want all of my brides to have an enjoyable, relaxing experience. I'm more than happy for them to try on whatever they want, but I also have a good eye for pulling out the unexpected dress which I know is going to look great.

What are your top 3 tips for choosing the perfect wedding dress?

- *Be open minded! Try on different styles even if you don't think they'll suit you, you might be surprised!*

- *Ignore size labels! Bridal sizes are often completely different to usual dress sizes. Most dresses will need some alterations, and can normally go up or down a size or two. The most important thing is that you look good in it.*
- *Make your dress your own! By saving on the cost of buying a brand new, made to order dress, you can add your own touches to make a truly unique dress. From adding a corset with coloured ribbon or some beautiful appliqué, dip dyeing or simply accessorising you can have a designer dress with bespoke details, making it truly unique to you.*

Number 1 piece of advice for a stress-free wedding day?

Relax! All the planning is done and what will be will be. Things may go wrong on the day, but that's life! The day will go so fast so make sure you take a breath, stop and actually enjoy it!

What don't people usually know about your job that you wish they did?

You need very strong arms! Being tall with long arms also helps! Wedding dresses are heavy and I am often lifting them off the rail, occasionally overhead and onto mannequins.

What info do brides need to know when they're looking to choose their wedding dress?

If you know your venue already, then this might help you choose the style of dress best suited. A beach dress won't be the best for York Minster, and a full length ball gown may be just too much for a destination wedding.

Think about whether you are having a classic wedding or more boho style, for example. Many dresses are suitable for all sorts of weddings, so apart from that, it just comes down to your own taste and style.

What should brides bear in mind when choosing dresses?

Remember that most dresses will need some alterations, so don't forget to budget for that. If you already have your shoes, bring them! Nude underwear is better, but most dresses have some level of inbuilt corsetry, so a bra is not normally needed. Don't wear fake tan or lots of make up as they risk marking the dresses.

How far in advance should brides be arranging their dresses?

At Bridal Reloved our dresses are bought "off the peg". We've even had brides come in during the week who are getting married at the weekend! We wouldn't recommend leaving it that late in case alterations are needed, but unlike dresses that are made to order, you can come in fairly close to your wedding date.

The best thing about this is that you haven't had time to go off your dress (we've had brides come in who no longer like the dress they ordered 2 years ago!) and it means you can find a dress that suits your body shape as it is, not worry that it may no longer fit.

Photographs by Jenny Milner Photography
Dresses by Bridal Reloved York.
Bouquets are by Ecoblooms -
Models are Chloe Markham of the Yoga Revolution and Tara Bailey of Dreamee Teepees
Chloe's floral crown is by Hare and Howl Floristry.

SUITS

https://www.jsshirts.co.uk/
https://www.instagram.com/jensonsamuelshirts/
https://twitter.com/jsshirt
https://www.facebook.com/JSShirt

Jenson Samuel is a premium provider of wedding suits in the Skipton and North Yorkshire area. We encourage our customers to embrace their individuality, rather than falling into the common trap of adhering to repetitive societal norms. We offer a vast selection of high quality shirts, ties and suits, specifically designed for those who wish to avoid the tedious, traditional black or navy stereotype and instead desire a high quality suit that will be remembered.

Additionally, we understand the considerable stress that goes into organising a wedding and therefore, we aim to make the process as stress free as possible. We provide a flexible, simple fitting service, complemented by the provision of refreshments. Furthermore, the variation in our collection ensures that whether you're an exuberant individual looking for an exotic outfit, or an introverted individual searching for a suit to match, Jenson Samuel is the provider you're looking for.

Top 3 tips for choosing your perfect wedding suit.

- *Remember to make the groom stand out. From shoes and ties to shirts and pocket watches, we have a variety of subtle details that we can incorporate to allow the groom main focus on the day.*
- *Co-ordinate with your bridesmaids. Accessories are the perfect way to pull the bridal party together.*
- *Location matters & match your surroundings! For example, if you're planning on getting married abroad, think lightweight, summer colours - a 2-piece perhaps. For a winter wedding, think warming tones with autumnal tints.*

Photo by Eyesome Photography - www.eyesomephotography.com

Number 1 piece of advice for a stress-free wedding day?

Planning is key. Sort what you can well in advance and don't leave anything to the last minute if you want to avoid those last minute stresses.

What don't people normally know about your job that you wish they did?

We love our job, but it comes with a lot of hard work and dedication. Everyday is different and every wedding unique. All of it is worth it though when we get to see the happy couple following their big day.

What info do couples need to know when they're looking to choose their wedding suits?

The Wedding Date & budget are the two most important factors to have pinned down prior to your initial fitting.

What should couples bear in mind when picking suits?

- *The style & theme of the wedding - you need to in-keep with the atmosphere you're trying to create. This could be anything from peaky blinders to traditional, shabby chic to star-trek (yes we've done it all!)*
- *Colour schemes.*
- *Number of groomsmen*

How far in advance should couples be arranging their suits?

We usually recommend an initial fitting with the all the groomsmen approximately 4 months in advance, with the outlook for a final fit about 4-6 weeks prior to the wedding day.
Saying this we've worked with parties who have had less than 3 weeks to go so anything is possible at Jenson Samuel!

CAKE

www.bellaroobakes.com
Email: bellaroo.bakes@gmail.com
Facebook: Bellaroo Bakes
Instagram: bellaroo_bakes

I'm Beth Booker, I trained and worked at The Langham, a 5* hotel in central London, for 8 years under one of the most renowned pastry chefs in the country. During this time I started doing most of the cake orders that the hotel received, and discovered how much I loved doing this over anything else. In 2016 I left the busy London life and set up my own cake making business from home. I make celebration cakes of any kind; birthdays, anniversaries, baby showers and weddings take up the majority of the orders. My favourite part of the job is how no two days are the same. I rarely get the same order twice, except for unicorn cakes, so every day is a new challenge to discover how to bring to life the creations my customers envisage. I pride myself on making bespoke cakes for any occasion.

What are your top 3 tips for choosing the wedding cake of your dreams?

- *Choose the flavours that you and your partner want, don't try to please everyone as you never will.*
- *Have something meaningful to you. If you like quirky things,*

and want cartoons or fresh flowers (or, like me, an aeroplane) on your cake then go for it. Trends will always be changing so don't feel pressured to go the traditional route either.

- If you would like a big cake effect but don't need 4 tiers worth of cake to eat, consider adding a 'bluff' cake layer. This is a fake cake that can be covered and decorated like the rest of the cake but it can often cut costs and still give that grand effect. Alternatively, if you have a tight budget, you can also opt for a smaller cake but add a few 'cutting bars' which will give you more cake but save on decoration and the labour costs of a bigger cake.

Number 1 piece of advice for a stress-free wedding day?

Enjoy every minute of it! Plan and organise as much as you can in the lead up to the day and make sure your organiser and any suppliers knows any specific or important requests. When the big day arrives, trust that it will all fall into place, and relax. Not everything will go to plan, so don't expect it to.

What don't people normally know about your job that you wish they did?

How long it can take to make seemingly simple decorations! For example, adding sugar flowers to an order rather than real flowers can drastically increase the labour time and, therefore, the price. Some flower decorations have to be made and then dried out in parts over several days before being assembled into the beautiful flowers you see at the end.

What info do couples need to know when they're looking to book a cake supplier?

As soon as you have a date and a venue I would get in touch with a few cake suppliers, have a rough idea of guest numbers and prices even if you don't know your design, flavours or theme yet. If you find a supplier whose style you absolutely love and you know it is within your budget, get your date pencilled in and come back to the design details when you are ready. Most suppliers will require a deposit to secure your date. Closer to the event I would be looking to know;

- *Where the cake is going to be positioned,*
- *if they have any cake stands you can use (if you desire),*
- *and what time your supplier will be able to access the venue to be able to assemble or add any finishing touches.*

What should couples bear in mind when picking a cake designer to work with?

I would encourage couples to have a cake tasting before securing your date. There is nothing worse than a beautiful looking cake that tastes dry and disappointing. I would also consider how far they are based from your venue so you can factor in delivery and set up fees. Most importantly I would pick someone that is willing to listen to exactly what you want, and who offers you lots of options for design and flavours. If you have an exact design in mind, that's great - if you like parts from 6 different cakes, that's also great. Your cake designer should be able to look at all the ideas you have and pull them together into something unique for you. But remember to listen to their advice too, they usually have a pretty good idea of how things will end up looking.

How far in advance should couples be booking you?

I would always ask for as much notice as possible, the more time you have, the more choices of suppliers and design you will have. Ideally, 6 months to a year. However, the bigger the company, the earlier you may need to book. Some will have much longer lead times. Always ask though! There might be a last-minute cancellation. I have done one order from tasting to wedding in the space of 2-3 weeks.

CELEBRANT

Yvonne Beck
ivvey@hotmail.com
+447800543426
https://celebrantinlondon.co.uk/
https://www.facebook.com/YvonneBeckCelebrant/
https://www.instagram.com/celebrant_yvonne/

Eleanor and Sam Wedding - Kevin Watkins Photography - www.kwphoto.co.uk

I love storytelling, and offering couples lots of choice when It comes to their special day, and as a Wedding Celebrant I am able to do just that! I came to this role after being introduced to a Celebrant in Australia, when I was a wedding guest at a beautiful ceremony held in a mountain top vineyard overlooking the ocean. It was a moment I will never forget, and eventually the time was right to begin this new chapter in my own life.

I trained with the Fellowship of Professional Celebrants, whose founder Terri Shanks was herself trained by the person who set up Celebrancy in Australia over 45 years ago! It has been a wonderful role that I have loved since I trained in 2011, and now, 175 or so ceremonies later, I love being able to be a part of such a milestone occasion as a Wedding, Vow Renewal, Naming, or indeed any special occasion that allows people to create lasting and meaningful memories.

What are your top 3 tips for creating your perfect wedding ceremony?

- *Think about your ceremony style, and go for it! With a celebrant, there are no restrictions! We love authentic, personal, and even fun or quirky, so find a celebrant that understands your style, ideas and can create a ceremony that's all about you!*
- *Book your Celebrant as early as possible – and definitely after you have looked at your venue! A Celebrant can use licenced or unlicensed spaces, and of course private homes and gardens too – but we only conduct one ceremony on any date, so it is important to book as early as possible to avoid any disappointment. With a Celebrant, you can consider booking the non-traditional days as we are happy to work 7 days a week!*
- *Think about the way you want to feel on your wedding day – your ceremony is the heart of that day, and the reason you are all together, so think about ways to involve your guests, perhaps by asking them to take part in a joint ceremony or activity which they can all engage in. I love new customs and rituals such as a ring warming, where the rings are passed to every person and they are asked to warm them with their love and good wishes. This is also a lovely moment for those who wish to say a prayer or blessing quietly. An independent celebrant will, in most cases, also be happy to include religious content – hymns, prayers, readings, blessings – so if you wish to blend faith, spirituality and custom and tradition, or create new customs (a signature cocktail perhaps, or a handfasting that involves all your family)- then just ask, as I am sure your Celebrant would love to create exactly what you dreamed of!*

Number 1 piece of advice for a stress-free wedding day?

As a couple who have asked for a Ceremony that is about them, I would say the most stressful part for them is often the Vows and Promises. This is where many couples feel they need to create some masterpiece and go for an Oscar – but in reality this is a quiet moment, where you look into each other's eyes and say what's in your heart. So my advice is - don't panic or rush your Vows – many couples are worried about speaking in front of their guests, and my advice is to rehearse them, don't make them too long or complex, and read them from a card so that you don't suddenly go blank. A Celebrant led ceremony should be relaxed, happy, full of smiles and allow you as a couple to truly be present with each other. So don't worry about where to stand, whether to stand or sit, whether to hold hands or not, whether to kiss each other or not, the main thing is to be able to feel comfortable, relaxed, and excited in the happiest of ways! Everything you do is going to be just fine!

What don't people normally know about your job that you wish they did?

I think couples are surprised at just how much we like to say YES! There are literally no restrictions, and we often find that the traditional church or register office services give the impression that it's all set in tablets of stone. Well, for a Celebrant led ceremony, you have exactly what you want in terms of format, content, location, size and time and length. I'm a bilingual Celebrant and offer ceremonies in English and German, and so this adds another opportunity for couples to be imaginative (German wedding customs are quite cool!) and creative (each partner choosing to say their vows in their partner's language rather than their own). A venue can be anywhere - the beach, woodland, a barn, a manor house, at home, in a local park, in a forest, nothing is off limits! So a couple really can plan to make their dreams a reality!

Nicole and Trung Queens House - photo by Kate Nielen Photography - www.katenielen.com

What info do couples need to know when they're looking to book a celebrant?

A venue does not have to be licenced for weddings if you are asking a Celebrant to create your ceremony. It is not a legal ceremony and therefore has no rules attached in terms of content and location. Many venues are licenced and will suggest a Registrar but that may come with restrictions you don't want to have at your wedding – your music, vows, readings etc. will be vetted, and any religious or spiritual content will not be allowed. My couples tend to have a standard registration at their local Register Office a day or so beforehand where they complete the paperwork for a legal marriage (much like registering a birth) and don't even need to exchange rings or vows if they prefer to do this in their Celebrant led ceremony.

As I said earlier, we often only conduct one wedding per date, so months like June, July and August are booked up quickly. It is possible however to obtain great rates at venues on off peak days like Monday or Thursday.

Consider booking your Celebrant as soon as possible, and let your photographer know – Celebrant ceremonies are wonderfully visual and creative, and your photographer will want to know key moments, to capture the excitement and joy of everyone who is taking part!

Tami and Sam at Shotley Vineyard Suffolk, photo by Nicholas Wallace

What should couples bear in mind when picking a celebrant to work with?

There are many kinds of Celebrants, and it is important to choose the right one for you. So shop around – not necessarily based on price, but based on whether this is the person you trust to create the centrepiece of your wedding day. Do they "get" you and your vibe? Are they properly trained, experienced, insured and do you feel that you can relax and work with them in a productive, and enjoyable way? Experience and skills do matter, as much, if not more than merely the price they are charging.

How far in advance should couples be booking a celebrant?

My couples tend to book me when they are booking their venue, so between 1 and 2 years ahead. Ideally around 12 months is great!

MAKE UP / HAIR

https://www.chryschapman.com/
mua.chryschapman7@gmail.com
07912372609
https://www.instagram.com/mua_chrys.chapman/?hl=en
https://www.facebook.com/ChrysChapman/

My name is Chrys. I moved to Harrogate from Malibu, CA (via Bath), so am now a Yorkshire-proud, mum of 2, entrepreneur (and I always spell that word wrong). I'm a freelance makeup artist, hair stylist & beauty/ massage therapist, specialising in creating beautiful, looks for my clients that make them feel like themselves, on their very best day. I believe that everyone is beautiful, and as my first makeup idol/ mentor Laura Mercier always says, what makes you unique, makes you beautiful. I like helping my clients accentuate their natural beauty, no matter how dramatic their makeup look is.

My passion is in creating and inciting transformation, and with my Bridal clients and their bride tribes I do that through hair and makeup. I also work with other hair and makeup artists with similar values, so that we can offer the same outstanding results to all of our clients.

What are your top 3 tips for getting your perfect wedding hair/make up?

- *Invest in your skin* - At the beginning of every trial I ask A LOT of questions, mostly centred around the look the bride is trying to achieve, but also about her skin. Getting to know a bride's skin is really important, because it determines how certain products will sit on the skin, what ingredients I need to avoid, and which products I will use on the big day. I always offer to send my brides a list of recommended skincare products and suggestions that they can invest in before the big day to get their skin into tip-top shape. I can do a great makeup, but to really get the most out of the application, your own skin being at its best is essential.

- *You are what you eat* - Brides don't need any extra pressure to lose weight, so let's get clear on this. I'm not saying to cut calories. What I am saying is eat mindfully. Caffeine, refined sugars, alcohol... they're all inflammatory on the gut, which means they're inflammatory to your skin, your hair, your body in general. Feed your body with things that are good for it and your skin will thank you. This doesn't mean deny yourself of all the treats. Far from it! But let them be treats, and let the bulk of your fuel come from foods that serve you. What happens in the gut, happens to your skin.

- *Try before you buy* - not all hair and makeup artists operate the same way with bookings, prices and policies. If you are in contact with a stylist/ artist who doesn't insist on a trial, I would be very careful. I have only ever attended a bride without a trial on one occasion, and that was because she'd been let down at the last minute by another HMUA. In addition to getting the style and results right, you have to know that you get on with that person. My job is an incredible privilege, and I appreciate so much that my brides welcome me into their most intimate and special time getting ready to say I Do. The chemistry you have with that person should be whatever you want it to be. My personal style is to be one of the bridal party. I've been known to shed my own tears when my brides get into their dress (even more when they do the big reveal with their dads... it's ALWAYS the dads). The relationship you have with your HMUA is important. Don't underestimate it.

Photo by Steph Simmons Photography -
www.stephsimmonsphotography.co.uk/

Number 1 piece of advice for a stress-free wedding day?

Call in the Avengers. Ok, you might not need Iron Man, but trust me, you'll want the best people on your team.

Preparation is key, but being able to let go of control is even better. I'm a planner -- a meticulous one. Give me a job, and I'll have a spreadsheet, graphs and research ready for you within a week. So I get it. You're planning a really big event and you want everything to be perfect. The thing is no one person can DO all the jobs and do them really well, so recruit the experts -- the suppliers who are going to be your dream team on your day. The people you KNOW will do the job you've hired them to do because they care so deeply about it that the thought of disappointing you cuts them deep. I've been doing this job for a while now, and I still struggle to sleep the night before a wedding, convinced I'll miss my alarm and run late or forget a bride's lipstick. The best way to enjoy your day is assemble your wedding Avengers.

What don't people normally know about your job that you wish they did?

It takes A LOT of hours from enquiry to wedding to really look after a bride. I hear the complaint ALL THE TIME.

"Why is it that as soon as someone says wedding/ bridal the price jumps so much?!"

I totally get where you're coming from. It feels unreasonable to absorb such a big sticker shock when all I'm doing is painting your face or playing with your hair. Let me say right now, I'm not just painting your face or playing with your hair. I'm investing in you. I invest in the right tools and products, I sacrifice my family time, I spend hours and hours in correspondence, marketing to find you, and in additional training -- all so I can be ready for you. If I can achieve your ideal result in an hour or two, it's because it's taken me lifetime to get to this point. Can you get hair and makeup cheaper? Sure. It's all a matter of priorities.

Also, we hair and makeup people are an absolute wealth of knowledge when it comes to other local suppliers! We know everybody, so if you're still looking for someone for another part of your wedding, ask! If we know, we'll tell you. And we'll usually have a fun story to tell you, too.

What info do couples need to know when they're looking to book a hair/make up artist?

Definitely Wedding Date. You'd be surprised how many enquiries I get without a date. We can start a conversation about service without a date, but I couldn't secure a booking without it.
- *Wedding Date*
- *Getting Ready Location*
- *Ceremony Start Time*
- *Time to get from Getting Ready Location to Ceremony Location*
- *Ceremony Venue*
- *Ideal Start and Finish Times (this will have an impact on how many artists will be required on the day)*
- *The Number of People in your Party*
- *Which services are required*

- *Ideally I suggest the bride has chosen her dress before her trial.*

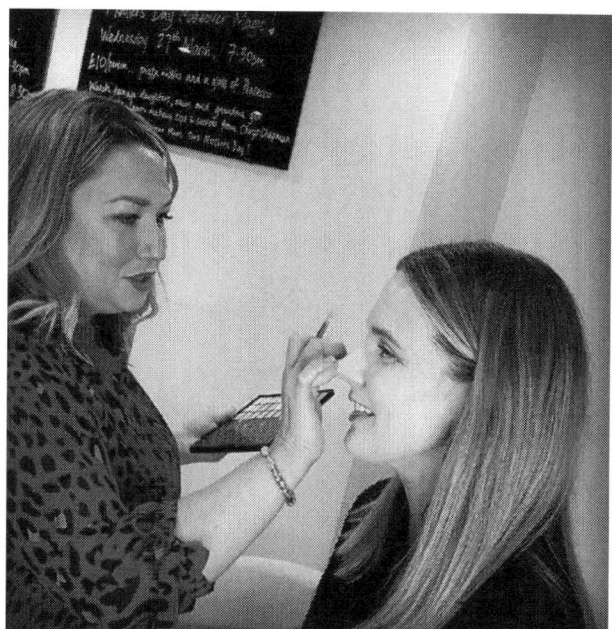

Photo by Steph Simmons Photography -
www.stephsimmonsphotography.co.uk/

What should couples bear in mind when picking an HMUA to work with?

I think it's important to remember that a HMUA is not just another invisible supplier, this is the person you are choosing to allow into your inner sanctum of wedding prep. They have to know their stuff, from product knowledge to expertise in the field, but being a part of your tribe is something you can't create a simple tick box for. Many of my couples find that choosing a photographer and choosing a HMUA is a similar process because of how much we are enmeshed in your day.

The other thing I would advise, is to ask your HMUA if there are any additional services they can offer. For instance, because I'm beauty / massage trained, I often do a pamper party a day or two before the wedding for the bride and her squad to do nails, possibly tans and brows. This gives me another opportunity to interact with the group, so that by wedding morning, if there had been any tendency to awkwardness, poof! Like magic! We are old friends. Equally, on the day, I'm happy to offer additional services like staying after the ceremony for touch up or setting up a Beauty Bar for the evening do. It's often the case with suppliers like a band or musician, that booking a bit of extra time actually works out more cost effective than you would imagine, because they're already there with you.

How far in advance should couples be booking an MUA?

If you've found someone whose work you follow and like, I would say waste no time in trying to secure them. Some of my dates 2 years from now have already gone to brides who I've connected with at Wedding Fairs. You can usually secure your date with a deposit, and book a trial much later once some of your bigger items have been booked. This is especially true for weddings in the high season. I think we used to only see June, July and August as high season, but for me my high season runs from April through to October. So don't delay.

That said, even if your date is only a few weeks away, don't be afraid to reach out to see if your ideal supplier has availability. Don't ask, you don't get. Even if they are booked, often they'll have recommendations on suppliers they would trust in their place.

THANK YOU FOR READING

This book has been a labour of love, and I really hope it helps you keep your wedding journey as stress-free and enjoyable as possible. I have so many regrets, both from my wedding day and in the run up to it, and if this helps just one person find way to the wedding they really want, then it's been worth me writing it.

This book was my first foray into non-fiction, and I could not have done it without the help of all the wonderful suppliers featured in Section Three.

Resources

You can find a full list of resources on the website here, including pdf copies of the worksheet and the checklist:

https://giftast.com/how-to-plan-your-perfect-wedding

FB group

Join the Facebook Group to chat with other brides and exchange tips.

https://www.facebook.com/groups/planyourperfectwedding

Mailing newsletter

Sign up to the Giftast Newsletter for 10% off your wedding stationery.

https://giftast.com/newsletter

ABOUT THE AUTHOR

Wedding Stationer Katherine Holt is on a crusade to beat wedding stress. In her new book, How To Plan Your Perfect Wedding: A Stress Free Guide To Designing Your Big Day, Katherine shares tips and tricks learned from running her own wedding business, and a previous role as a top Exec PA. Find out more at www.giftast.com.

Katherine also writes gothic historical fiction, based in and around Leeds and Lincoln. She has a lifelong love of Regency historicals, and a developing interest in mental health and psychopathy. Katherine's writing grows steadily darker and moves further away from glittering ballrooms and deeper into the seething gloom of the human mind.

Her first book, His Wicked Shadow, was released in May 2014, followed by An Unnatural Daughter in December 2014.

The Liberty Troupe Trilogy, book one of which was released in early 2015, is a Regency mystery set in and around Leeds in 1814. Read more at www.misshwrites.co.uk, where newsletter subscribers can download a free Liberty Troupe short story.

ALSO BY THIS AUTHOR

His Wicked Shadow

When the elderly and wheelchair-bound Earl of Lincoln is found unconscious in the rain, nobody can understand how he got there. Seven years later, his son falls to his death amid rumours of madness. Aged just 19, James Elliot is forced to shoulder the burden of the title, and all it carries with it.

Elinor Montague has been in love with James since they were both children. She helped him as he mourned his father and grandfather, and if he occasionally acted a little strangely, she was prepared to ignore it. After a few glasses of champagne at a masked ball, things heat up between Ellie and James, and she's convinced it's love. He, on the other hand, runs off to Europe the following day and doesn't come back for two years.

When James tries to woo the newly wealthy Ellie on his return, a string of strange accidents begin to befall them both. While she tries to remain aloof, Ellie finds herself drawn to James once more, but refuses to give in until she finds out what he's hiding– and solves the mystery of the shadow that has hung over his life.

An Unnatural Daughter

Fleur Mason and her father have never been close.

At his request she marries Gabriel Raynor, but after only three days she flees her new home, leaving her husband for dead. Taken in by Edwina and Tristan Lovett, Fleur finds happiness with the family she always wished for, until her father staggers back into her life. He's been badly beaten, and pleads for her to return to her marital home, where a scarred Gabriel awaits, seeking vengeance.

The cost of Gabriel's forgiveness is one life, Fleur's or her father's. Now Fleur must decide who will pay.

The Liberty Troupe Trilogy

The Review

Evelyn Thompson isn't much of an actor, but she's an expert at keeping a stiff upper lip. When The Liberty Troupe are asked to perform for the Duke of Wellington, it seems like the chance of a lifetime. Their last production was a disaster, but with The Yorkshire Advocate covering everything from preparations to performance, a good review could mean big things for the troupe. But the pressure puts a strain on the players' already fragile relationships. Evelyn is struggling to stay on civil terms with her alcoholic mother, and her artist father seems to have picked up a troublesome commission. Then there's the reporter who's been assigned to the story - he's terribly handsome, but he's asking some strange questions… As opening night looms, pretending everything is going well won't be enough. The Review is the first book in The Liberty Troupe trilogy, set in Leeds in 1814.

The Governess

You don't choose your family. Sometimes a family can choose you.

When Evelyn Thompson's father is murdered, her life falls apart. When it looks like her mother is the culprit, it seems impossible to pick up the pieces.

Bent on revenge, Evelyn applies for the position of governess at the home of Brendan Fitzroy, her mother's lover. In spite of her lack of qualifications, she is taken on for a two week trial.

As she meets more members of the Fitzroy family, it looks like Evelyn isn't the only one with an ulterior motive.

The Advocate

MURDERESS AT LARGE! £5,000 REWARD!

In this, the final instalment of the Liberty Troupe Trilogy, Evelyn must battle with more than just her conscience as she discovers the line between right and wrong is more blurred than she thought.

They're already calling her a murderess, and with no way to prove her innocence, Evelyn Thompson might as well become just that.

Printed in Great
Britain
by Amazon

32399790R10077